Christmas Book

8 Jazzy Piano Solos with
Optional CD Accompaniments

Arranged by Mike Springer

Jazz music is fun to play year round, especially at Christmas time. From driving swing to jazz waltz, the *Not Just Another Christmas Book* series has it all. The carefully crafted arrangements are perfect for Christmas parties and recitals, or they can be used simply for fun.

Additionally, the books are truly unique because they contain accompanying CDs that feature bass and drum parts to create the sense of playing in a jazz trio. Each tune has three different CD tracks in the following order:

* For listening, the *Performance Model* track features the piano, bass, and drums in a complete performance.

* For practicing, a *Practice Tempo* track features the bass and drums (without the piano part) at a slow tempo.

* For performing, the *Performance Tempo* track features the bass and drums (without the piano part).

For practice and performance ease, a two-measure drum lead-in is given at the beginning of every CD track. Metronome marks for both tempos are given at the beginning of each arrangement.

Contents

For my mentor and friend, Dr. Jerry Wallace

Produced by
Alfred Music Publishing Co., Inc.
P.O. Box 10003
Van Nuys, CA 91410-0003
alfred.com

Printed in USA.

ISBN-10: 0-7390-8116-0
ISBN-13: 978-0-7390-8116-7

Cover photos
scizzors cutting paper: © istockphoto.com / hatman12 • ribbon: © istockphoto.com / egal • Christmas wrapping: © istockphoto.com / fotoAta

Go Tell It on the Mountain

1 Performance Model
2 Practice Tempo (♩ = 100)
3 Performance Tempo (♩ = 144)

Traditional
Arr. Mike Springer

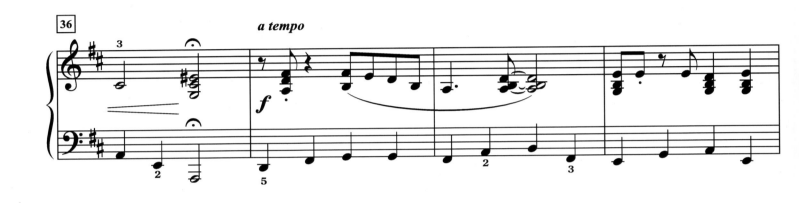

God Rest Ye Merry, Gentlemen

4 Performance Model
5 Practice Tempo (♩ = 92)
6 Performance Tempo (♩ = 132)

Traditional
Arr. Mike Springer

O Holy Night

7 Performance Model
8 Practice Tempo (♩ = 76)
9 Performance Tempo (♩ = 100)

Music by Adolphe C. Adam
Arr. Mike Springer

Let It Snow! Let It Snow! Let It Snow!

10 Performance Model
11 Practice Tempo (♩ = 100)
12 Performance Tempo (♩ = 132)

Music by Jule Styne
Arr. Mike Springer

Ukrainian Bell Carol

13 Performance Model
14 Practice Tempo (♩ = 120)
15 Performance Tempo (♩ = 176)

Traditional
Arr. Mike Springer

We Three Kings of Orient Are

16 Performance Model
17 Practice Tempo (♩ = 92)
18 Performance Tempo (♩ = 120)

Words and Music by
John H. Hopkins, Jr.
Arr. Mike Springer

Joy to the World

19 Performance Model
20 Practice Tempo (♩ = 76)
21 Performance Tempo (♩ = 108)

Music by G. F. Handel
Arr. Mike Springer

Spirited, with a funk groove

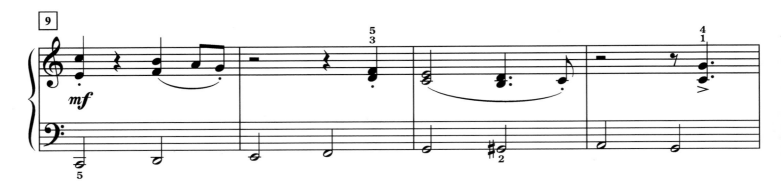

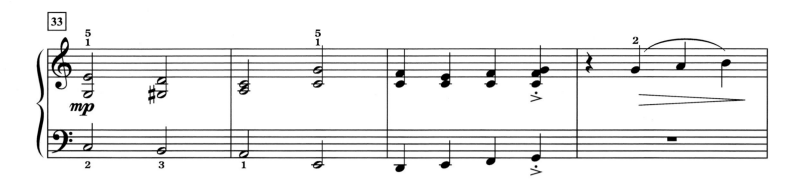

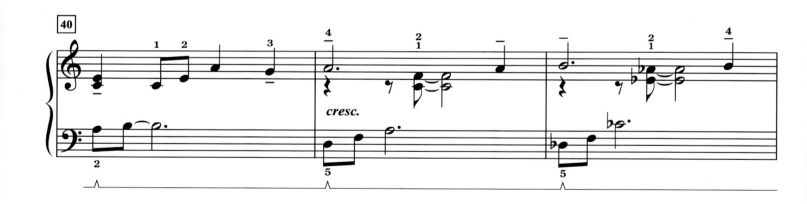

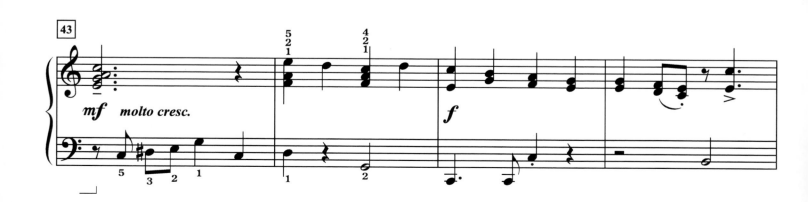

I'll Be Home for Christmas

22 Performance Model
23 Practice Tempo (♩ = 52)
24 Performance Tempo (♩ = 60)

Music by Walter Kent
Arr. Mike Springer